Welcome to The Nativity, Jesus is Born Coloring Book.

Happy Christmas to you. We are very happy that we can experience Christmas with you by recollecting scenes from the lives of Jesus, Mary, and Joseph.

Inside there are 29 pages for your child to color it, all hand illustrated. You can cut out each illustration and frame it if you want. Coloring develops your child's manual skills and creativity. Most of all, your child gets to know the world while playing.

I recommend using fine-tipped markers, colored pencils, watercolors pencils. All can be found at any local craft store or online shop. A heavy application of paint can make the paper buckle a bit so. If you decide to use markers, there is a "cut-out-page" at the end of the coloring book that you can use as an insert between the pages in case of bleed-through. Remember, coloring should be good fun. So enjoy!
Thank you so much

Ana

C000045598

design by Lullanka

design by Lullanka

design by Lullanka

design by Lutianka

design by Lullanka

Cut this page and use as a pad

If it's not a problem for you, I would greatly appreciate if you could leave your feedback in review on Amazon once you're finished reading, our team want to create a better and more beautiful product for you.

Visit our Author Page on Amazon.

Lullanka Design

Printed in Great Britain
by Amazon